W9-ASL-391

DATE DUE			

Holidays and Culture

Islamic Holy Month

by Terri Sievert

Consultant:
Council on Islamic Education
Fountain Valley, California

Capstone *press*

Mankato, Minnesota

First Facts is published by Capstone Press,
151 Good Counsel Drive, P.O. Box 669, Mankato, Minnesota 56002.
www.capstonepress.com

Library of Congress Cataloging-in-Publication Data
Sievert, Terri.
    Ramadan : Islamic Holy month / by Terri Sievert.
    p. cm.—(First facts. Holidays and culture)
    Summary: "A brief description of what Ramadan is, how it started, and ways people
celebrate this cultural holiday"—Provided by publisher.
    Includes bibliographical references and index.
    ISBN-13: 978-0-7368-5392-7 (hardcover)
    ISBN-10: 0-7368-5392-8 (hardcover)
    1. Ramadan—Juvenile literature. 2. Fasts and feasts—Islam—Juvenile literature. I. Title.
II. Series.
    BP186.4.S54 2006
    297.3'62—dc22   2005015590

Editorial Credits
Jennifer Besel, editor; Juliette Peters, designer; Wanda Winch, photo researcher; Scott Thoms,
    photo editor

Photo Credits
Art Directors/Jeff Greenberg, 7
Capstone Press/Karon Dubke, 13, 16, 21
Corbis/Atef Hassan/Reuters, cover, 14; Ed Kashi, 4–5; Kamran Wazir/Reuters, 9; Reuters, 10,
    18–19; Sygma/Parrot Pascal, 17
Corel, 1
Getty Images Inc./Jed Jacobsohn, 20
PhotoEdit Inc./Mark Richards, 6

1 2 3 4 5 6 11 10 09 08 07 06

Table of Contents

Celebrating Ramadan

As the sun sets, a family sits down to a meal. Everyone is very hungry. No one in the family has eaten all day. They have been **fasting** for Ramadan.

Ramadan is an **Islamic** holiday. During this holiday, **Muslims** honor their faith and **culture**. Going without food reminds families to be thankful for all they have.

What Is Ramadan?

Ramadan is the ninth month in the Islamic calendar. Muslims use this month to refocus their minds on God.

For the whole month, Muslims focus on God by fasting and praying.

Another important Ramadan **custom** is helping the poor. Muslims collect food and money to give to the needy.

Fact!

Muslims use a calendar based on the moon. Ramadan begins about 11 days earlier each year. One year Ramadan may begin in January. Ten years later, it will begin in September.

A Special Visit

Muslims believe that hundreds of years ago a man named Muhammad received a special visitor. An angel appeared to Muhammad, bringing messages from God.

Muhammad took God's words and put them in a holy book called the **Quran**. Today, Muslims try to read the entire Quran during Ramadan.

Fact!
The Quran is written in the Arabic language. Allah (al-LAAH) is the Arabic word for God.

10

Watching for Ramadan

Before the angel's visit, Ramadan was simply the ninth month in the year. But today, the month is a time to focus on faith.

When the first **crescent** moon of the month appears in the sky, Ramadan has begun. Families stay up late to watch for the moon. Some people even climb on their roofs to get a better view.

Fact!

In some countries, people fire a canon when the moon is first spotted. This lets everyone know Ramadan has begun.

The Fast

The Quran teaches Muslims to fast during Ramadan. During the whole month, Muslims do not eat or drink while the sun is out.

Fasting is a custom that shows Muslims how it feels to have little food. They learn what poor people go through. Saying no to food also helps Muslims learn to control their actions.

Fact!
Some people don't fast because it might hurt their health. Young children, pregnant women, and the elderly are not expected to fast.

Breaking the Fast

Before the sun rises in the morning, families get up to eat a meal called the *suhoor* (su-HOOR). This meal has to fill them up. They won't eat or drink for the rest of the day!

When the sun sets at the end of the day, families gather to break the fast. They eat a meal called the *iftar* (if-TAAR).

Fact!

Muhammad broke his fast by eating dates. Families follow this custom today to honor Muhammad.

Eid al-Fitr

The end of Ramadan brings a big celebration. This festival, called Eid al-Fitr (EED all-FIT-er), is a fun time for families. Children get gifts of clothes and money.

Communities hold carnivals with rides and games. But most importantly, Muslims thank God for helping them through the fast.

A Time for Faith

Muslims fast and pray to devote themselves to God. Focusing on God and all he's done is the most important part of Ramadan.

All around the world, Muslims fast and pray during Ramadan. Together, they honor their culture and faith.

Fact!

Ramadan is a special time to focus on faith, but Muslims try to serve God all the time. They pray five times a day all year long.

Amazing Holiday Story!

Hakeem Olajuwon is a former NBA superstar, and he is also a Muslim. In 2001, Ramadan came during some important games for Olajuwon's team. He didn't want to let his team down, but he also wanted to follow his faith. So, Olajuwon did not eat or drink during the day. He was tired, but he played hard. His team won the games and Olajuwon was able to share his faith with others.

Hands On: Collection Jar

Ramadan is a time to help those in need. You can make a collection jar to gather money for the poor.

What You Need

tissue paper   water
glue   small paint brush
small bowl   wide-mouth jar

What You Do

1. Tear the tissue paper into strips.
2. Put a small amount of glue in a bowl. Mix in just enough water to make the glue runny.
3. Spread glue on the jar with the paint brush.
4. Place pieces of tissue paper all around the jar.
5. Spread another layer of glue on top of the paper with the paint brush.
6. Let the jar dry.
7. Use your jar to collect money for those in need. You can donate the money to a local food shelter to help feed hungry people in your town.

Glossary

crescent (KRESS-uhnt)—a curved shape; a crescent moon looks like a sliver in the sky.

culture (KUHL-chur)—a people's way of life, ideas, arts, customs, and traditions

custom (KUHSS-tuhm)—a tradition in a culture or society

fast (FAST)—to give up eating and drinking for a period of time

Islam (iss-LAAM)—a religion based on the teachings of Muhammad

Muslim (MOOS-lim)—a person who follows the religion of Islam

Quran (kur-AAN)—a holy book used by followers of the religion of Islam

Read More

Hoyt-Goldsmith, Diane. *Celebrating Ramadan.* New York: Holiday House, 2001.

Walsh, Kieran. *Ramadan.* Holiday Celebrations. Vero Beach, Fla.: Rourke, 2003.

Internet Sites

FactHound offers a safe, fun way to find Internet sites related to this book. All of the sites on FactHound have been researched by our staff.

Here's how:
1. Visit *www.facthound.com*
2. Type in this special code **0736853928** for age-appropriate sites. Or enter a search word related to this book for a more general search.
3. Click on the **Fetch It** button.

FactHound will fetch the best sites for you!

Index